PIG APPEAL

PIG APPEAL

Laurie Platt Winfrey

Walker and Company ✳ NEW YORK

A Celebration of Swine

'The time has come,' the Walrus said
'To talk of many things:
Of shoes—and ships—and sealing wax—
Of cabbages—and kings—
And why the sea is boiling hot—
And whether pigs have wings.'

Lewis Carroll

For Robert Beahan Shnayerson and Mary Dawn Earley

Library of Congress Cataloging in Publication Data

Winfrey, Laurie Platt.
    Pig appeal.

    1. Swine.   2. Swine (in religion, folk-lore, etc.)   3. Swine in art.
4. Swine in literature.   I. Title.
SF395.4.W56   1981   700   ·80-51853
ISBN 0-8027-0668-1
ISBN 0-8027-7166-1 (pbk.)

First published in the United States of America in 1982 by the
Walker Publishing Company, Inc.

Published simultaneously in Canada by
John Wiley & Sons Canada, Limited, Rexdale, Ontario

Cloth ISBN: 0-8027-0668-1
Paper ISBN: 0-8027-7166-1

Library of Congress Card Number: 80-51853

Designed by Joyce Cameron Weston

Printed in Hong Kong by South China Printing Company

10 9 8 7 6 5 4 3 2 1

Pigs have never enjoyed a good press. But for those unthinking legions who would malign the pig, there have always been those prescient few who have made it their business to celebrate the worthy hog in literature and in art.

The pig has been described by Homer and Virgil, by Dylan Thomas and George Orwell. It has been painted on Greek vases, drawn by Rembrandt and Rubens, illuminated in manuscripts, fashioned by toy makers. It appears as banks and weather vanes, in children's stories and movies. The pig is smart, humorous, subtle, and sexy whether in the lowliest barnyard or in the elegant boudoir of Miss Piggy. For all those who have celebrated swine, none has succumbed more lovingly to the sublime appeal of *pig* than G.K. Chesterton:

The actual lines of a pig (I mean of a really fat pig) are among the loveliest and most luxuriant in nature; the pig has the same great curves, swift and yet heavy, which we see in rushing water or in rolling cloud. Compared to him, the horse, for instance, is a bony, angular, and abrupt animal . . . There is no point of view from which a really corpulent pig is not full of sumptuous and satisfying curves . . . He has that fuller, subtler and more universal kind of shapeliness which the unthinking (gazing at pigs and distinguished journalists) mistake for a mere absence of shape . . .

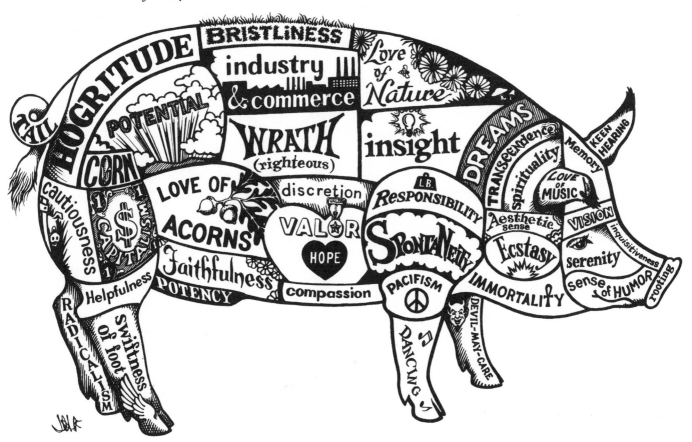

Collared
peccary

White-lipped
peccary

Daedon: Extinct
pig ancestor

Bushpig

Warthog

Wild boar

Babirussa

Forest hog

Ancestors

The pig family tree has roots some thirty-six million years old. Beginning in the Oligocene epoch with the giant pig *Elotherium* as pictured by Charles Knight *(right)* the pig-like mammals split into two families: the Peccaries, which live in the southwestern United States and throughout South America, and the Old World pigs, which live in Africa and Eurasia. From the Old World wild boar descend all the varieties of the domestic pig.

Man's first artistic representation of the boar *(below)* was found in the caves at Altamira in northern Spain and has been carbon dated at 13,500 B.C. These extraordinary animal cave paintings were produced as part of a Paleolithic ritual to ensure a successful hunt.

10

In Ireland the pig is described as "the gentleman who pays the rent," and as far back as the early Iron Age when the bronze boar *(right)* was fashioned, Ireland was called *Muic-inis*, or Pig Island. The boar's great strength and ferocity, which inspired the striking figure *(opposite, above)* caused it to become a cult object in many early cultures. In Celtic mythology the boar or pig was a supernatural being with prognostic powers, and a harbinger of death and disaster. What better companion in arms could an early warrior take to battle than a representation on his helmet of the mighty boar? *(opposite, below)*

More pacific in spirit were the Egyptians, who cast the sow nurturing her piglets as an animal sacred to the sky-goddess Nut *(below)*.

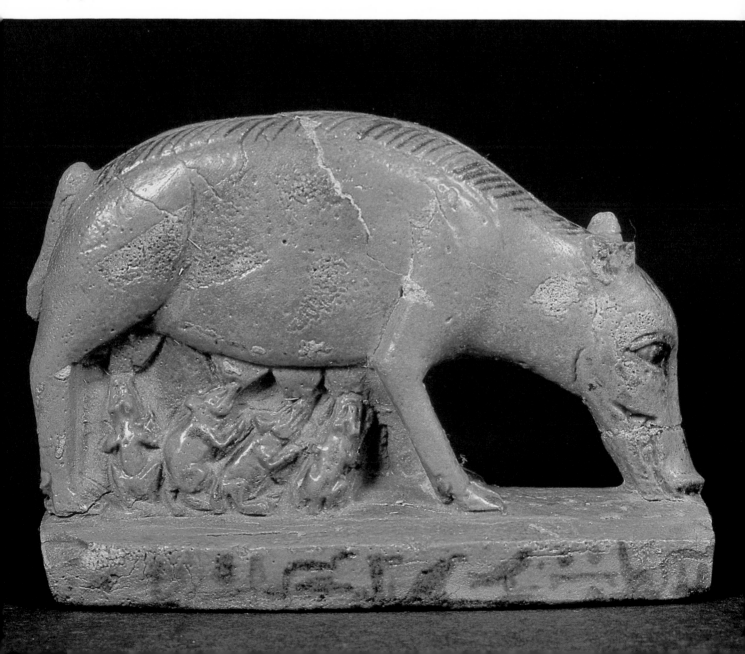

The Classic Pig

When Greek artists were painting pigs and other animals on vases, they were illustrating stories and legends. Meleager tackles the Calydonian boar on the krater *(below)*, and a pig is sacrificed to Demeter, the goddess of agriculture *(left)*, as punishment for ravaging her crops. The most striking examples of Greek pig art come from an anonymous Attic artist known as the "Pig Painter". His exquisite pelike *(opposite)* shows Odysseus and his swineherd Eumaios with his pigs—belying the saying found in both Greek and Roman literature, "You cannot make a silk purse out of a sow's ear."

. . . as when a mountain boar,
Bold in his might, abides the
oncoming rout,
In lonely spot—bristles his ridgy
back,
His eyes blaze fire, his tusks he
whets the while,
All eager to beat back both dogs and
men.

Homer, *Iliad* XIII

Homer wrote the world's first account of a boar hunt centuries before Christ. The figures from Hellenic mythology slipped easily into the Roman pantheon. A third-century B.C. sarcophagus repeats the theme of Meleager and the Calydonian boar *(below)*. More secular aspects of man's quest for the wild hog are shown in mosaics *(opposite)* made 600 years later for the Royal Palace of Piazza Armerina in Sicily.

In the *Aeneid*, Virgil tells how
Aeneas was advised to build his
new city in Italy on a site where he
would find a great white sow
suckling thirty piglets. A symbolic
representation of the beginning of
Rome *(opposite)* now resides in the
Vatican Museum. Less portentous
is the bronze group *(above)* of the
domestic animals usually found
in the second-century Roman
barnyard.

Pigs of the East

In Imperial China the pig symbolized good luck in business. As early as 5000 B.C., when the pig was first domesticated, it occupied a valuable place in the Chinese economic hierarchy. Models of the pig were placed in the hands of the dead as hopeful porcine symbols of prosperity in the next world *(left)*. More majestic representations were also included in tomb artifacts, such as the bronze plaque from the Han dynasty *(below)*. That the pig's closest relative is the hippopotamus was not lost on the modeler of the heavy-snouted fellow on the opposite page below; nor on the wicker pig above him, which nonchalantly carries a model of itself on its back.

18

Vishnu, the dominant god of
modern Hinduism, embodies in
himself many separate gods or
avatars. In his incarnation as Va-
rahavatara the cosmic boar *(opposite)*, Vishnu is shown rescuing the
beautiful earth-goddess from the
primeval ocean and gently lifting
her towards a heavenly assembly of
gods and sages. Varahi, one of the
seven mother-goddesses and the
female aspect of Varaha, holds the
earth-goddess in her lap while
devouring a fish *(below)*.

Beautiful Boars

The artistry of the fifteenth-century Milanese illuminator is the real subject of the painting opposite. That he has portrayed a boar hunt is incidental to his extraordinary mastery of design. Five hilltop towns and a fat white rabbit overlook a stylized hunting scene that includes whimsical hunters in proplike trees, the sleekest dogs to ever approach a boar, and a pastoral enclosure of feeding deer. The boar and the bloody goings-on are lost in the setting. Everyone from the great Mogul nature painters *(above)* to Henri Rousseau owes a debt to the anonymous Italian miniaturist.

Two vignettes from a thirteenth-century bestiary *(right)* show and tell of the differences between "Porch de la nature" and "domestic porch."

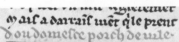

24

Acorns

The illuminators of medieval Books of Hours enlivened their lists of saints with seasonal scenes of feudal life. The Labors of the Months might depict a September grape harvest or March ploughing; November was reserved for pigs and acorns. French pigs had a passion for acorns and might still if the truffle detail had not taken over. These miniatures from the Books of Hours of the Duc de Berry (*opposite*), of the Duchess de Bourgogne (*below*) and of Jeanne d'Evreaux (*right*) all show bucolic scenes of peasants and their pigs in the forest.

From Oak to Oak they run with
*   eager haste,*
And wrangling share the first
*   delicious taste*
of fallen ACORNS; yet but thinly
*   found*
till the strong gale has shook them
*   to the ground.*
It comes; and the roaring woods
*   obedient wave:*
Their home well-pleased the joint
*   adventurers leave.*

Robert Bloomfield
The Farmer's Boy

Prodigal Son

"Neither cast ye your pearls before Swine" warned the Apostle Matthew in the *New Testament*. Early Christianity's disdain for the pig carried over to the Parable of the Prodigal Son who, before his return to the family fold, reached the low point of his exile as a swineherd among the symbolically unclean. The pigs are used to emphasize the depths to which the second son had sunk by reason of his own profligacy and waste. The scene has been imagined by Albrecht Dürer *(opposite)* and by an anonymous sixteenth-century English embroiderer *(above)*.

27

In Renaissance Europe big and small game were no longer hunted primarily for food. The sport of kings in the 1545 Cranach painting of a hunting party in honor of Charles V *(below)* included deer, bear, a fox and rabbit as well as boar. The king in the lower left corner seems somewhat removed from the complicated spectacle going on behind him. The hunters in these other sixteenth-century scenes have not underestimated their quarry and come equipped with nets, spears, bearers and dogs.

Pigs of the Artist

(pp. 30-31) Den-Den, a 450-pound Yorkshire sow living on a Pennsylvania farm, struck her owner's fancy. The felicitous coincidence that her owner was the artist James Wyeth resulted in this four- by seven-foot still life portrait. According to William Hedgepeth, Wyeth became "purely enamored" of Den-Den, finding her eyes "so human . . . like a Kennedy's." During the course of the sitting, the artist's model downed seventeen tubes of oil paint. For the next week there were rainbow droppings wherever Den-Den went.

Copyright © 1970 by James Wyeth.
Private collection.

"Fatness itself is a valuable quality. While it creates admiration in the onlookers, it creates modesty in the possessor . . . Nor do I mean that mere fatness is the only beauty of the pig. The beauty of the best pigs lies in a certain sleepy perfection of contour." Some fairly eminent onlookers have agreed with G.K. Chesterton over the centuries and have made their own versions of pig-perfection—Pisanello's drawing *(opposite, above)*, Rubens's pen and ink *(opposite, below)* and the etching by Rembrandt *(above)*.

"Beauty," says the lettering on the improvised pig shelter in Adolf Dehn's watercolor *(below)* "is where *you* find it." Both Dehn and the British artist Stanley Spencer have found it in the farm scenes on these pages. With his brush, Dehn has transformed a rather ramshackle barnyard into a pleasant and humorous pastoral, while Spencer has endowed "Ricketts Farm, Cookham Denn," *(opposite)* with the quintessential ambience of the English countryside. Contributing hugely to the charm of both watercolors is the appealing presence of their pigs.

The first artist to perfect a body of work with the pig as the central character was George Morland, who was active in the late seventeen hundreds and who created the pigs here. Chesterton might have had his fellow countryman's sketch (*right*) in mind when he lamented, "Tears of regret come into my eyes when I remember that three lions or leopards, or whatever they are, sprawl in a fantastic foreign way across the arms of England. We ought to have three pigs *passant* . . . It breaks my heart to think that four commonplace lions are couched around the base of the Nelson Column. There ought to be four colossal Hampshire hogs to keep watch over so national a spot."

Feeding the barn animals was a distasteful business in Rowlandson's late eighteenth century *(above)*. Small wonder they ate like pigs. But help was on the way. By 1858 Farmer Johnson had devised a patent hog trough which made mealtime more pleasant for both the diner and the maître d' *(right)*. Before setting the pigs out for summer feeding, "it was necessary to ring their snouts to prevent them rootling up the meadow *(opposite)*. This is an ear-splitting task, for though their snouts are callous, pigs always squeal as soon as handled, and their voices have a note which vibrates the human ear drum to the point of physical pain."* A pig squeal can reach 115 decibels, three higher than a Concorde may produce during a restrained takeoff.

*Adrian Bell, *The Cherry Tree*

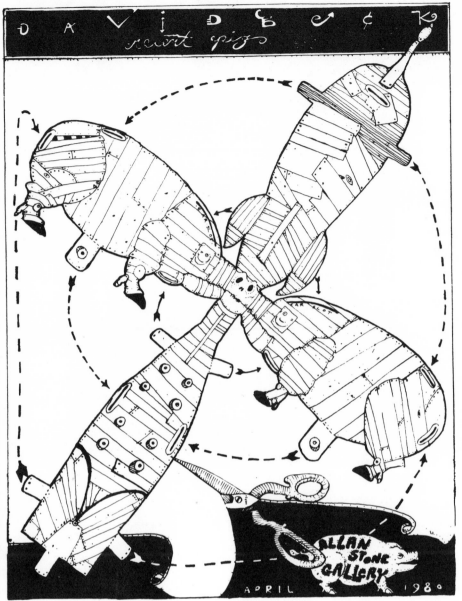

In a Pig's Eye

David Beck's six-foot-long pig (*opposite*) is constructed of wood implanted with hog bristles bought from a brush manufacturer and inserted one at a time. Impressive as it is from the outside, the real spectacle begins when the tail is turned. The eyes fall in and the side slats roll up to reveal a miniature drive-in movie complete with cars with lit headlights, a chorus line, and musicians playing bongo drums beneath two movie screen lovers. Over all, a moon casts a blue glow. *In a Pig's Eye* took eight months to complete.

Alexander Calder made his sow (*below*) out of wire in 1928.

This Little Piggy Went to Market

A democratic beast
He knows that his . . . drivers seek
Their profit, and not his.

Robert Southey, 1799

The Farmer John–Clougherty
Meat Packing Company is proud to
be the only meat packer in the West
who gets live pigs from the Midwest
corn belt for their slaughterhouse in
Los Angeles. They are also proud of
the whimsical scenes of pig country
life that are painted on over a mile
and a half of the plant's walls, some
of which are shown here and on the
following pages.

Of course, the unseen activities
inside the plant offer a sharp
contrast to the high life pigdom just
outside.

The painting is popular; it is on
the art bus tour organized by the Los
Angeles Museum and also attracts
weekend gawkers who more than
once have bumped fenders while
making the mile-and-a-half circuit.

43

The Farmer John mural was conceived and begun in 1957 by Les Grimes, an Australian who was painting Hollywood sets for a living. He began the mural by painting a hundred-foot section of the wall, and added another and then another until finally the entire plant was covered in pigs enjoying the highest delights that pigdom can offer. For ten years Grimes perfected and maintained his mural. Then in 1968 while restoring a section fifty feet above the ground, he fell from the scaffolding and was killed. Arno Jordan *(left)*, an Austrian artist, has since that time worked year-round restoring and adding to the first and still most important piece of American Big Art.

P. H. MILLER

DRY.   GOODS

D. BEANS.

The Performing Pig

The pig is the only animal other than man capable of thinking through a problem to a rational solution—the dictionary definition of intelligence. Pigs can therefore not only be trained to do anything a dog can, but they will learn the task in a shorter time. All the pig has to do in the nineteenth-century trade sign *(opposite)* is to pull a pig cart with Uncle Sam and a steaming pot of baked beans. Beans, salt pork, molasses and brown bread—what could be more American? Well, possibly the American Indian pig mask *(above)*.

In the early English toy *(below)*, a young lad rides his prize pet bareback.

LITERAL & SCHOLASTIC

Pigs have a penchant for performing. They can quickly learn how to dance, pull carts, be ridden, retrieve and compete in races. Their sense of smell enables them to sniff out truffles twelve inches under the ground at distances of twenty feet. Unfortunately, the exquisite rarity of the truffle is also appreciated by the pig and some hard negotiating occasionally occurs.

The normal life span of a pig allowed to age gracefully is fifteen to twenty years. In the one year allotted the some seventy-five million pigs raised annually for the market in the United States, the pig can hardly even approach its intellectual potential. Remove a pig from the market cycle and he will prove to be capable of the amazing feats shown by the "troupe of very remarkable trained pigs" who per-

formed with the circus in 1898 (*opposite*). Unlike the old dog or racehorse, the old hog is rarely rewarded for his service with a peaceful retirement. As Toby, the Learned Pig, laments:

In this world, pigs as well as men,
  Must dance to fortune's fiddlings,
But must I give the classics up,
  For barley-meal and middlings?

Oh, why are pigs made scholars of?
  It baffles my discerning,
What griskins, fry and chitterlings
  Can have to do with learning.

Alas! my learning once drew cash,
  But public fame's unstable,
So I must turn a-pig again
  And fatten for the table.

Thomas Hood, *The Lament of*
Toby, the Learned Pig

49

Pig Tales

Pigs get a bad press but never more so than when an adult decides to use them to show *human* behavior to children. Pigs are themselves neither bourgeois, petty nor lecherous, but their reputation of "behaving like swine" was established by the unthinking long before Jean Grandville gave his least savory characters the heads of outsized hogs.

XXXVI

Ma femme est sortie, ma petite chatte...

That pigs have made their way into literature is evidenced by the publisher's logo *(left)*.

Illustrators drawing the pig as a foil for their human subjects sometimes unintentionally instilled in him more charm and intelligence than the people around him. *The Three Jovial Horsemen* combined *(opposite)* don't look like a match for the pig-perfection at their feet.

Slovenly Kate *(below)* is a totally tiresome child who would not even qualify as a handsome pig . . .

So she set the little creature down, and felt quite relieved to see it trot away quietly into the wood. "If it had grown up," she said to herself, "it would have made a dreadfully ugly child; but it makes rather a handsome pig I think—." And she began thinking over other children she knew, who might do very well as pigs . . .

Lewis Carroll, *Alice's Adventures in Wonderland*

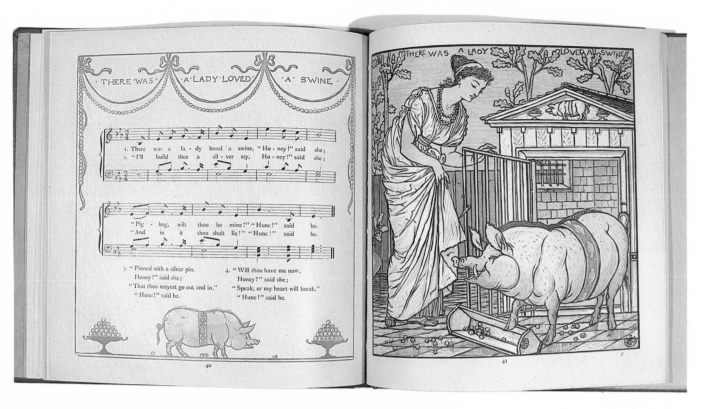

Finally, two English illustrators drew the pig in all its diversity. Walter Crane made a charming illustration of the pig as "object of desire" for the poem about a lady who loved a swine *(above)*. Equal to Walter Crane as an illustrator of children's books was Randolph Caldecott. What plump pigs he has drawn to illustrate *The Farmer's Boy (opposite)*, precursor to *Old Macdonald Had a Farm*; and what child or adult could resist his dancing pigs *(left)* in the familiar nursery rhyme, "Hey, diddle diddle, the cat and the fiddle, the cow jumped over the moon"?

Jogging Pigs

It's not easy to be a pig or to be an animal whose physiological and psychological similarities to man are surpassed only by the primates. The pig's skin, metabolism and heart structure are most like man's and the pig tastes good—so either way, the pig loses. New York artist Angela Fremont, whose paintings appear here, is in her third year of pigs. She became interested in the subject after seeing a television news spot on jogging pigs. The pigs were jogging twenty-five miles a week so researchers could see if spontaneous collateral circula-tion—increased blood flow—oc-curred consistently. It didn't.

In an Arizona study, pigs are jogging two miles a day to test the effect of jogging and high fat diets on heart problems. So far the

researchers have found that the jogging pigs are more energetic and cheerful than the sedentary ones. Small wonder, however, that today pigs, like people, are susceptible to stress and heart attacks.

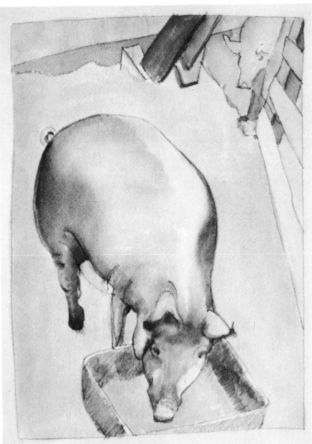

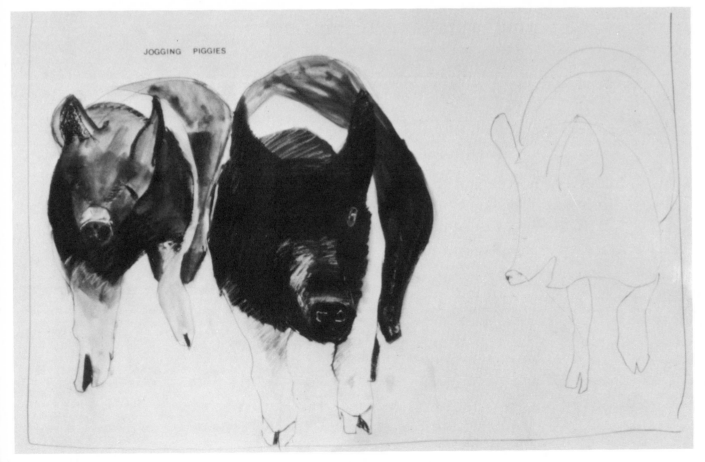

Children's Pigs

Beatrix Potter wrote *Pigling Bland* in 1913. One of the best loved of all pigs, Pigling *(left)*, with his engaging, slightly priggish character, could only have been created by one who look upon pigs with humor and affection. On the opposite page, below, is a scene from the MGM adaptation of Miss Potter's stories, *Peter Rabbit and Tales of Beatrix Potter*.

Today's children are as familiar with Miss Piggy *(below)*, femme fatale of the Muppets, as with any movie star.

In their roles as athletes, cartoon stars Porky Pig and his feminine friend display quite unporcine agility.

The Animated Pig

The animated pig is directly descended from the literary pig. Aesop's fables included the story of the three little pigs who foiled the wicked wolf by the hairs of their chinny chin chin. George Orwell's *Animal Farm (below)* is based on the intellectual eminence of pigs where, in the words of their leader, Napoleon, "all Animals are equal but some animals are more equal than others." The most felicitous pig in animation or literature is Wilbur, Charlotte the Spider's devoted friend in E.B. White's *Charlotte's Web (opposite).* "In the words of the spider's web, ladies and gentlemen, this is some pig."

HARPER'S WEEKLY.

A JOURNAL OF CIVILIZATION.

VOL. XVIII.—No. 911.]   NEW YORK, SATURDAY, JUNE 13, 1874.   [WITH A SUPPLEMENT. PRICE TEN CENTS.

Entered according to Act of Congress, in the Year 1874, by Harper & Brothers, in the Office of the Librarian of Congress, at Washington.

The Pejorative Pig

Piggish, pig-headed, hogwash, road hog, pork-barreling, pigsty . . . One of the more evocative references in the porcine vocabulary is the use of "pig" to describe an officer of the law. One might assume that the epithet was a product of the violence and confrontation of the nineteen-sixties as evidenced by the still from *Fritz the Cat (left)* and from the bemusement of the cops with their namesake *(below)*. Actually policemen and pigs were linked by the press as early as 1874. The drawing opposite, from that year, is by the famous nineteenth-century cartoonist Thomas Nast.

Fred McDarrah

63

The practice of avoiding the eating of pork was rooted in practicality, became a superstition and finally developed into full-fledged religious prohibition. Tacitus maintains that the Israelites did not eat pork because it carried a kind of leprosy, no doubt referring to trichinosis, a sometimes fatal, always debilitating disease contracted from under-cooked pork that carries the parasite.

The pig was valuable only to the settled farmer. The nomads, who felt superior to the farmer, came to despise the pig as well as the farmer who bred it. In due course, religious laws developed against the animal the nomads themselves could neither breed nor keep. Ironically, the world's largest pig farm (opposite and below, left) is in Kano, in northern Nigeria, where most of that country's antipork Muslim population is concentrated.

Ceremonial Swine

The African tribal mask is often a stylized zoomorphic composite of many different animals. It is possible in one mask to combine long, swept-back antelope horns with the warthog's bared teeth and short tusks. The mask from Liberia is made appropriately of warthog tusks and shotgun shells *(opposite, below)*. Originally used for ritual display, the real significance of many African masks has been lost in a decline of the traditional ceremonies and a willingness of the elders to accept Western interpretations.

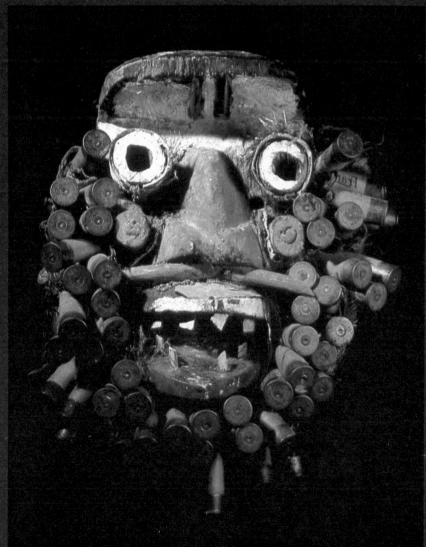

The Pacific Pig

Pig heaven is being a pig in New Guinea, which may account for the contentment expressed by the South Sea Island pigs on these pages. Pigs live in the family dwelling, are reared and even occasionally suckled by the wife. The *Moca*—a Pacific potlatch—is a ceremonial feast among New Guineans at the end of which the host gives valuable material goods, first among them a pig, to the guests.

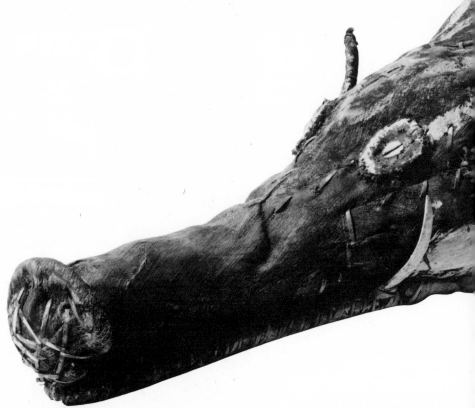

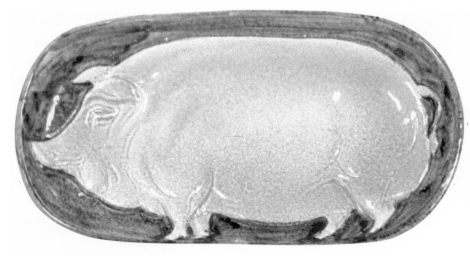

The Porcelain Pig

The very word "porcelain" is derived from the Italian *porcella*, or young sow. The particular elements of china seem to resemble closely the pink of the pig's skin—even when the pig looks like the RCA dog *(opposite, above)*. The Royal Copenhagen's rosy curiosity, the pink Italian porker and the sow and piglet waiting for their trough to be filled are happy examples of the match of material and subject.

The Glass Pig

Glass is the least common material in which the pig has been modelled. Somehow, the very earthboundedness of the pig—winged rumors to the contrary—mitigate against representing their stolid shapes in transparent crystal. The shapes of the nestled pair *(below)* and the boar *(opposite)* follow from the natural behavior of glass in its molten state. The squat glass pig *(right)* has four increasingly tiny pigs inside.

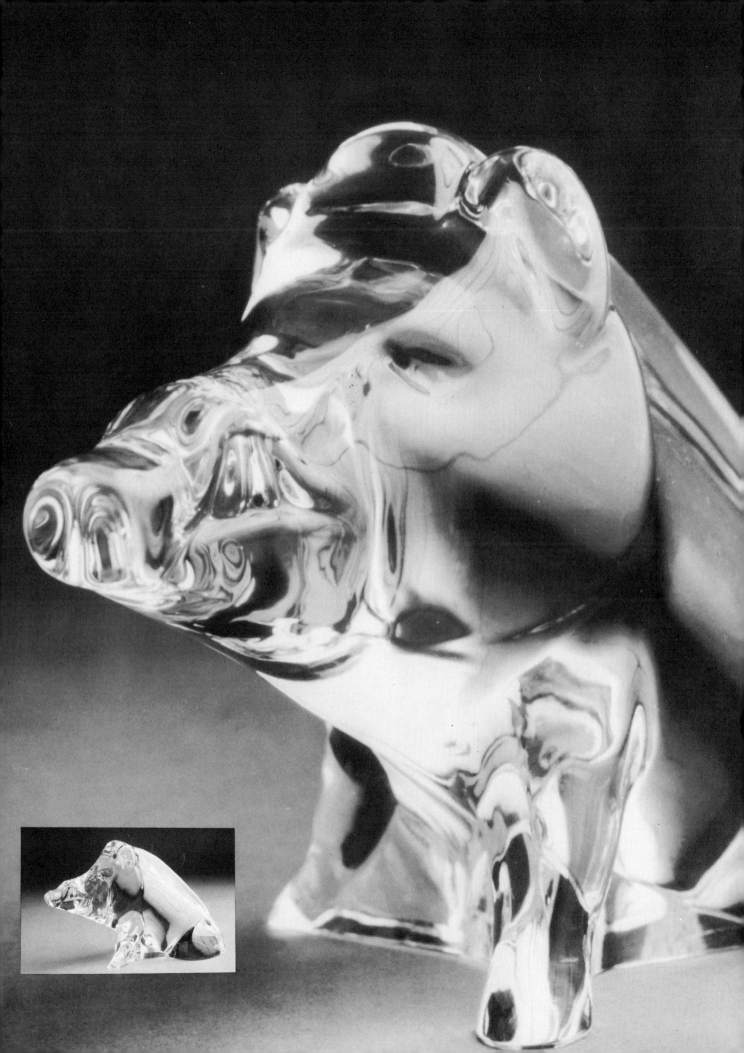

Sozzled Swine

'Twas an evening in November,
As I very well remember,
I was strolling down the street in
* drunken pride.*
But my feet were all a-flutter,
So I landed in the gutter,
And a pig came up and lay down by
* my side.*
Yes, I lay there in the gutter,
Thinking thoughts I could not utter,
When a colleen passing by did softly
* say,*
"Ye can tell a man that boozes,
By the Company he chooses"—
At that the pig got up and walked
* away!*

Contrary to popular belief, the pig does not overeat, nor can it be tempted to do so. It is, however, the only mammal other than man that will voluntarily drink enough alcohol to get drunk. Under a study described by porcophile Ken Britt, most alcoholic pigs consumed an average of one quart of 86-proof vodka daily. One pig—named Friendly for her willingness to tipple—set a farm record: Every day for a week she drank the equivalent of four quarts of vodka.

The nineteenth-century English drinking vessel (below) is a Sussex pig whose head doubles as a cup.

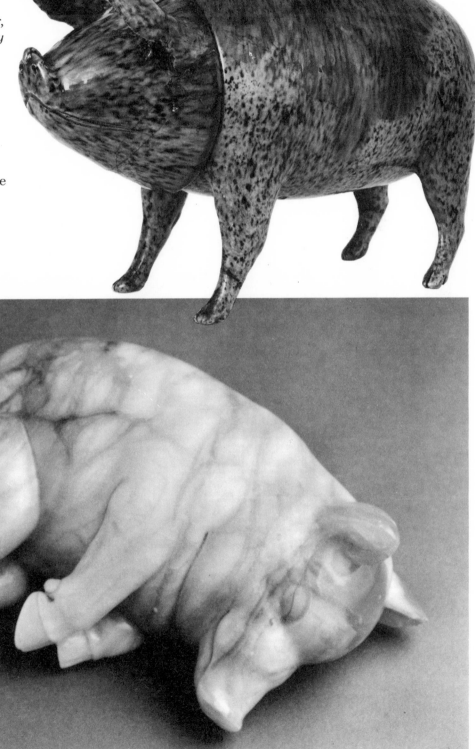

75

Wallowing

The sweat glands of a hog are woefully inadequate to their task. Thus, a hot hog must stay cool by immersing himself in the only bit of water at foot, which in a pigsty is more often than not a nice, gooey mud hole.

(*overleaf*)
Both the pert and rather smug domestic pig in overalls and the brightly colored Russian folk art toys attest to the possibilities for charm that lurk under the muddy hide of the common barnyard porker.

When little silk pigs from slumber
    awake,
Throwing off sleep with a frisk and
    a shake,
        Rosy and sweet.

Little pigs, rosy and thrilled to be
    free,
Wild with enchanting vivacity,
Sporting like children so gay and
    carefree,
        Are taut and clean.

Plump little bodies as pink as a rose,
Bare as the day they were born, I
    suppose,
Innocent cupids with neat little
    toes,
        And sly grimace.

Little pink pigs and none of them
    lean,
Patches like truffles on satin-pink
    skin,
More or less aping a nice galantine,
        Dappled with sun.

Tired little pigs, relaxed on the
    ground,
Curled up the claret-dark trough
    around,
Content and well-fed, with hardly a
    sound
        Rosily sleep.

Edmond Rostand
Les Cochons Roses

80

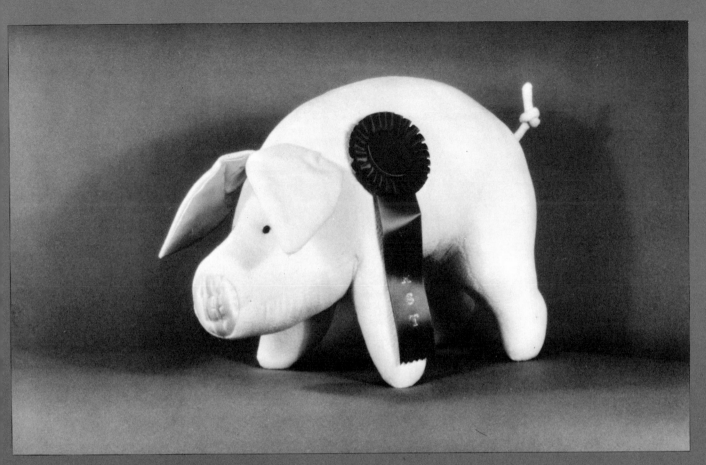

Piggies for Pennies

By far the most popular form the pig takes today—aside from Miss Piggy—is the venerable piggy bank. Very few have survived from early times because tradition called for breaking the bank—an expression nowadays associated more with the gambling circuit—when it was full of coins. Piggy banks like these from England, Mexico and Italy lend themselves to floral ornamentation.

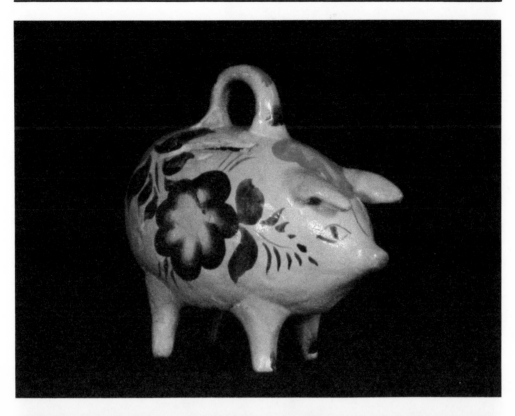

Household Pigs

A pig is more easily housebroken than a puppy. It is his eventual size that is usually the deciding factor in pig eviction cases. While the new 200-pound mini-pigs are dainty compared to your 800-pound hog, that is still a lot of pig to have around the house. The pig objects on these pages make pleasant alternatives to the real thing, and handy items in a porcophile's collection.

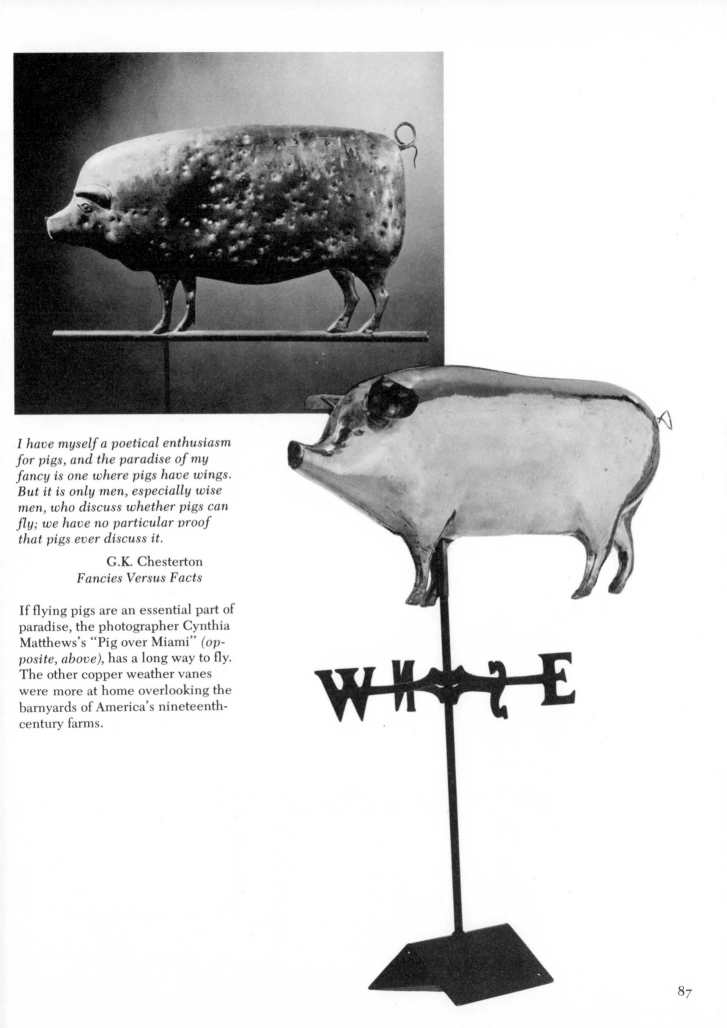

I have myself a poetical enthusiasm
for pigs, and the paradise of my
fancy is one where pigs have wings.
But it is only men, especially wise
men, who discuss whether pigs can
fly; we have no particular proof
that pigs ever discuss it.

G.K. Chesterton
Fancies Versus Facts

If flying pigs are an essential part of
paradise, the photographer Cynthia
Matthews's "Pig over Miami" (*opposite, above*), has a long way to fly.
The other copper weather vanes
were more at home overlooking the
barnyards of America's nineteenth-
century farms.

He is not suspicious, or shrinkingly
submissive, like horses, cattle, and
sheep; nor an impudent devil-may-
care like the goat; nor hostile like
the goose; nor condescending like
the cat; nor a flattering parasite like
the dog. He views us from a totally
different, a sort of democratic,
standpoint as fellow-citizens and
brothers, and takes it for granted,
or grunted, that we understand his
language . . .

William Henry Hudson
The Book of a Naturalist

Pritikin's Pigs

All alteration man could think,
  would mar
His Pig perfection.

  Robert Southey, *The Pig*, 1799

Robert Pritikin is a man who would
not dream of changing one hair on a
pig's chin. His celebration of swine
is centered in his San Francisco
hotel, where pig murals cover the
walls and porcophilia reigns su-
preme *(right)*. His nineteenth-
century French carousel pig domi-
nates one of the dining rooms. A
serious art collector with a sense of
the outrageous, Pritikin has con-
tinued his pigs in his nearby house.
Its front door is wired for
sound, so when it's opened, callers
are greeted by noises of birds
twittering, hogs grunting and a little
bit of down-home country music.

Pigskin

Pig leather breathes better than other leathers because, in life, the bristles extend clear through the hide, providing a pattern of air holes in the tanned skin. Not only is pigskin used for accessories like the pig stool *(opposite, below)*, but by placing sections of it on a burn victim's wounds, it helps relieve the torment of the raw nerve endings exposed to the air.

Although the boar seems to be getting the worst of it in the Japanese netsuke *(below)*, in fact the layer of fat beneath the pig's skin stops snake venom from reaching its bloodstream. Snake is a delicacy on the pig's catholic dinner menu.

Hog bristles are commonly used in hairbrushes—more unusual is an early American ivory pig comb *(opposite, above)*.

(overleaf) The pig's loyalty, modesty, quick wit, playfulness, ingenuity and charm are all evident in the nineteenth-century manuscript from Thailand. The man leaves his wife for a day's work in the forest, happens upon a drowning pig whom he rescues and carries tenderly back to his house to nurture. The following page shows the woodsman at work while his pig gambols nearby, the pig offering his assistance in measuring the teak. Finally, work done, the two admiring companions head back to the forest.

92

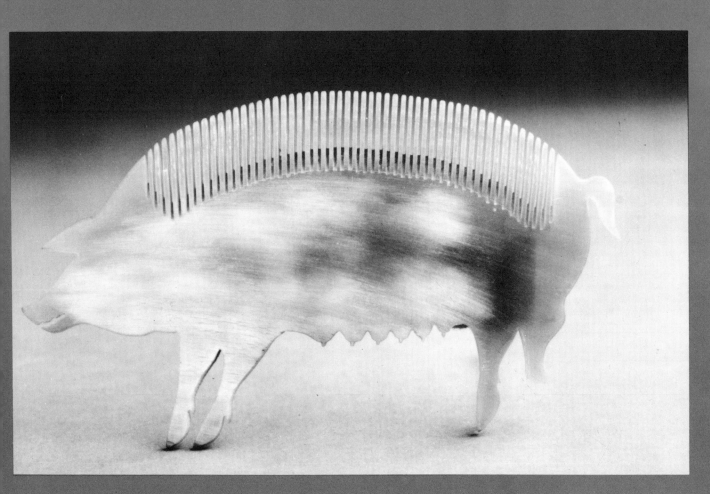

หลวง พ่อ พัด
ไม่ ได้วาน
พบ ลอง
เทยุ้นัน

จุคารวะวัง

Acknowledgments

I am particularly grateful for the generosity of Robert Pritikin and Mary Dawn Earley. In addition, I would like to acknowledge the help of the following people in the preparation of this book: John Blaustein; Woodfin Camp; Oberto Gili; Irwin Glusker; Mary Hilliard; Charlie Holland; Arno Jacobsen; Rosemary Klein; David Mercer at Hog Wild; Andrea Nasi; Robert Rainwater, Joseph Rankin and Betty Roth at the New York Public Library; Rosanna Rossi; Carey Winfrey.

Illustration Credits

The following abbreviations are used:
  BM—British Museum
  FM,C—Fitzwilliam Museum,
    Cambridge
  (MH)—Photograph by Mary Hilliard
  MMA—Metropolitan Museum of Art
  MOMA—Museum of Modern Art
  NYPL—New York Public Library
  RP—Collection Robert Pritikin—
    Photograph John Blaustein/Woodfin
    Camp

p. 2: Courtesy Laughing Giraffe (MH); **p. 5:** © John Findley from William Hedgepeth, *The Hog Book* (Doubleday & Co.); **pp. 6-7:** Janet Beller; **p. 9:** (top) Museum of Natural History (bottom) Musée de l'Homme, Paris; **p. 10:** (top) Louvre (EPA) (bottom) Helmet, Torslunda, Sweden, 8th century, Museum of Antiquities, Stockholm (Photoresources); **p. 11:** (top) Iron Age boar, National Museum of Ireland

(bottom) glazed pottery, 600 B.C., BM (Michael Holford); **p. 12:** (top) Archives Photographiques, Paris (bottom and **p. 13**) FM,C; **p. 14:** Capitoline Museum, Rome; **p. 15:** (both) (Fabbri Editori); **p. 16:** MMA, Rogers Fund, 1909; **p. 17:** Vatican; **p. 18:** (top) Brooklyn Museum (bottom) bronze from tomb, district of Tsing-ning, China (Giraudon); **p. 19:** (both) RP; **p. 20:** Brooklyn Museum; **p. 21:** BM (Photoresources); **p. 22:** *Traites . . . de Veneri*, 15th century, Ms. 368, Musée Condé, Chantilly; **p. 23:** Bestiary, 13th century, Ms.Fr. 15104, Bibliothèque Nationale, Paris; **pp. 24-25:** (both) Musée Condé, Chantilly (Giraudon); **p. 25:** (top) MMA, Cloisters Collection, 1954; **p. 26:** BM; **p. 27:** Cooper-Hewitt Museum; **p. 28:** G. de Molina, *Libro de la Monteria*, 1582, BM; **p. 29:** (top) Sotheby Parke Bernet (bottom) Prado; **p. 32:** (top) FM,C (bottom) BM (Freeman; **p. 33:** BM (Freeman); **p. 34:** Tate Gallery; **p. 35:** Whitney Museum of American Art; **p. 36:** BM (Freeman); **p. 37:** FM,C; **p. 38:** (top) FM,C (bottom) New York Historical Society; **p. 39:** William Sidney Mount, *Ringing the Pig*, 1842, New York State Historical Association, Cooperstown; **pp. 40-41:** Courtesy Allan Stone Gallery; **p. 41:** (bottom) MOMA; **pp. 42-45:** (all) Courtesy Andrea Nasi (Oberto Gili); **pp. 46-47:** New York Historical Society; **p. 47:** (top) Museum of the American Indian (bottom) Bethnal Green Museum, London (Michael Holford); **p. 48:** Library of Congress; **p. 49:** NYPL; **pp. 50-51:** (all) J.J. Grandville, *Metamorphoses du Jour*, 1854, Prints Division, NYPL; **p. 52:** (top) RP (bottom) Theodor Hoseman,

Slovenly Kate, 1852, Free Library of Philadelphia; **p. 53:** R. Caldecott, *Three Jovial Horsemen*, 1880, Prints Division, NYPL; **pp. 54-55:** (all) Prints Division, NYPL; **pp. 56-57:** Collection of the artist; **p. 58:** (top) RP (bottom) (Steve Smith); **p. 59:** MOMA; **pp. 60-61:** (all) MOMA; **p. 62:** Library of Congress; **p. 63:** (top) MOMA (bottom) Fred McDarrah; **pp. 64-67:** (all) Museum of African Art (Eliot Elisofon); **p. 68:** RP; **p. 69:** (both) Brooklyn Museum; **p. 70:** (top) Collection Mary Dawn Earley (MH) (bottom) RP; **p. 71:** (top) (MH) (bottom) RP; **p. 72:** (top) Hog Wild (MH) (bottom) Courtesy Steuben Glass; **p. 73:** RP; **p. 74:** Library of Congress; **p. 75:** (top) FM,C (bottom) RP; **p. 76:** (top) A. Velde, *Swine Sleeping*, 1660, MMA, Havemeyer Collection (bottom) A. B. Davies, *Place of the Mothers*, Brooklyn Museum; **p. 77:** Walter Shirlaw, *Pigs and Chickens*, 1877, Cooper-Hewitt Museum; **pp. 78-79:** (both) RP; **p. 80:** Courtesy Royal Copenhagen (MH); **p. 81:** (top) Hog Wild (MH) (bottom) RP; **pp. 82-83:** (top) Collection Winfrey-Shnayerson (MH); **p. 83:** (bottom) Hog Wild (Winfrey); **pp. 84-85:** (all) Collection Mary Dawn Earley (MH); **pp. 86:** (top) Cynthia Matthews (bottom) Sotheby Parke Bernet; **p. 87:** (top) Museum of American Folk Art (bottom) Courtesy Hog Wild; **pp. 88-89:** Dorothea Lange, *By the Chinaberry Tree*, Tifton, Georgia, 1938, Oakland Museum; **pp. 90-91:** Courtesy Robert Pritikin; **p. 92:** BM; **p. 93:** (top) RP (bottom) Hammacher Schlemmer; **pp. 94-95:** Thai Ms. 49, 19th century, Spencer Collection NYPL; **p. 96:** Library of Congress

96